330 Reasons To Love The Corps

Silly, Serious and Revealing Reasons to Love the U.S. Marine Corps

Written and Compiled by Chris Lawson

Army Times Publishing Company
Springfield, VA

Army Times Publishing Company Book Division

Vice President:	Joseph A. Acerno
Marketing:	Diana Snyder
Promotion:	Bill Wilson
Assistants:	Nicola Faustino, David Porter
Design:	Dana Shamblin

Published by Army Times Publishing Company, Springfield, VA 22159

ISBN: 9-9647942-1-7

Library of Congress Catalog Number: 96-078537

Printed in the United States of America.

INTRODUCTION

Duty. Honor. Courage. Commitment. These are some of the reasons why America loves its Marines. Boldness, self-assuredness, and a well-known "can-do" attitude are still others.

For perhaps a thousand strange, serious and nebulous reasons, the American public has long held the legion of Marines in the highest regard. And generation after generation continues to place Marines high atop a pedestal.

For more than 221 years, phrases like "First to Fight", "Tell that to the Marines" and "Send in the Marines" have been constant reminders of public pride in the "Fighting Leathernecks."

Marines feel that way about themselves too. Their pride in who they are and the ideals they represent are obvious. It's unmatched by any other military service.

In some small way, I hope to convey some of the reasons Marines – and the American people they defend – are so proud of themselves and their Corps. I came up with a few more than 330 reasons, but the list, like the Corps itself, could go on and on.

The original idea for this project came about in 1994, the 219th birthday of the Marine Corps. As a tribute to the readers of the MARINE CORPS EDITION OF NAVY TIMES, the editors and I decided to do a cover story titled: "219 Reasons to Love The Corps." The response from our readers was so overwhelming that we decided to expand the concept in 1995. The idea for this book soon followed. Many of those original reasons, however, are included in this latest work.

Many Marines themselves – those of bulging biceps and jutting jaws – can't tell you why they love their Corps so much. But they do love it, almost to a fault. You could hit many of them upside their "jar" heads with an entrenching tool and they'd barely flinch. But play the Marine Hymn at a star-spangled, patriotic parade and they're likely to blubber like a baby. Their pride runs deep.

Listen up, Marines. Here are some of the reasons why you and your Corps are so special.

CHRIS LAWSON, WASHINGTON, D.C.
(USMC, 1985-1991)

Acknowledgements

Special thanks to Dana Shamblin for the inspiration and the constant push to keep going.

Thanks also to the creative, fun-loving crew at Navy Times who helped come up with many of the original "219 Reasons to Love the Corps" (Navy Times, November 1994): Tobias Naegele, Gidget Fuentes, Ernie "Blaze" Blazar, Jean Norman, Jack Weible, Sean Burke, Pat Pexton, John Burlage, Bill Stump, Jon Anderson, Sheila Ross, B.J. Ramos and Becky Garrison. In addition, thanks to the Marine Corps public affairs staff in Washington for their support and cooperation.

Most of all, thanks to all the people - Marines and civilians alike - who shared their stories, hearts and memories with me for this project.

For my parents, Jack and Phyllis Lawson. Thanks for your never-ending love, support and encouragement.

And to MGySgt. Renaldo R. Keene, USMC (Ret.) You taught me what it takes to be a writer as well as a Marine. You're one of the best.

1. Toughest mascot. The Marine Corps' is a bulldog. The Navy's: a goat.

2. Great slogans: "Once a Marine, always a Marine."

3. Chesty Puller. You gotta love a service that has heroes with names like that.

4. The Book of Remembrance. Stored at the post chapel at Quantico, it lists the name, rank and date of death of all Marines and sailors who served with Marines and who gave their lives in Vietnam.

5. MREs. You hate to love 'em, but when you're hot and sweaty and in the field, nothing satisfies like the beef frankfurters and beans.

6. Dress blues. They're the coolest uniforms in any military worldwide.

7. Bloused cammie trousers. Another distinctive Marine look that sets the proudest service members apart.

8. The rest of the Marine sea bag. From the Alphas to the camouflage utilities, uniforms just look better on a Marine than any other service member.

9. Sunrises at sea.

10. The Marines take care of their own. On the battlefield, nobody's left behind — dead or alive — and the homefront is always secure.

11. The ACE. The best card in any warfighter's deck.

12. Your first Expert Rifleman badge.

13. The birthday cake.

14. Humanitarian missions. From Haiti to Somalia, Marines are not just life-takers, they're also life-savers.

15. Navy beachmasters. You don't come ashore without them.

"Some people spend an entire lifetime wondering if they've made a difference to this world. The Marines don't have that problem."

— President Ronald Reagan, 1985

16. The Med.

17. The battle colors.

18. Mess duty (just kidding).

19. Field day. Thursday nights will never be the same.

20. The public speaking classes the Corps gives you: "SIR! Private Schmuckiteli requests permission to speak to Senior Drill Instructor Staff Sergeant Reyes, SIR!"

21. Rigid raiding craft.

22. Best phone number. Call 1-800-MARINES and you've got the Corps. And if you've got what it takes to be a Marine, a recruiter there will be happy to sign you up.

23. Value for your tax dollar. The Corps does it all for less — just 6 cents of every dollar spent on defense goes to the Marines.

24. Toughest boot camp — 12 weeks long, and about to get even longer.

25. Hashmarks. A salty sign.

26. Family Service Centers.

27. The Rock. Not Alcatraz, but OKI.

Chris Lawson

28. Marines in flight suits (so say the women in their lives.)

29. Former Marines. There's no such thing as an "Ex-Marine."

30. Every clime and place.

31. The CH-46 Sea Knight. Say a Hail Mary and climb aboard. Nobody makes 'em anymore, but Marine ingenuity keeps 'em flying. And with a safety record that's nothing short of a miracle.

32. PAOs: First to go, last to know.

33. Hot Shots. The award-winning Marine Corps Rifle and Pistol Teams.

34. Col. Charles Waterhouse and all the Corps' combat artists.

35. Holiday Routines.

36. You ARE a Marine. Not a soldier, or troop.

37. Marine training doesn't wear off. It lasts a lifetime.

38. The Stumps. A desert oasis for warriors.

39. The Island Hopping campaigns.

"It is a tremendous privilege for me to work with Marines and Marine recruits here at Parris Island. The hard work, motivation, dedication and love for the Marine Corps has rubbed off on me (plus put me in the best physical condition of my life). This might sound a bit like sweet talk, but, honestly, after three years on Parris Island, I still get goose bumps when I hear The Marines' Hymn."

— Lt. Jim Osendorf, Navy chaplain;
Parris Island, S.C., 1995

40. Friendships. Forged in training and battle, they last forever.

41. The intangibles. The sense of pride, confidence, achievement and belonging to something bigger than yourself.

42. Vertical envelopment. The Marines led the way.

43. PT cadences. The old ones, anyway.

44. The real meaning of the term MEU (SOC): Mail Excluding Units Stuck Off Coast.

45. Anodized brass.

46. Pogey-bait.

47. Moxy. "Tell that to the Marines."

48. Navy Landing Craft. Cadillacs they're not, but they get the job done.

49. Naval status. Sailors live and work on ships. Marines go for cruises — then hit the beach.

50. The Iron Mike statue at Parris Island.

51. Dining-Ins.

52. Service. The Marines have fought at more places than any other military branch.

53. Every officer is ready and capable to lead a platoon of Marines.

54. The 90 Navy ships that have been named in honor of Marines, past and present.

55. Style. The only service to have its uniform displayed in **GQ** magazine. Even with all its variations, the Marine uniform is clean. No bells, no whistles, all class.

56. First Lieutenant Sarah Deal. The Corps' first female pilot.

57. **LEATHERNECK** magazine. The enlisted man's bible.

58. **THE MARINE CORPS GAZETTE**. The officer's bible.

59. The **MARINE CORPS EDITION OF NAVY TIMES**.
Everyone's bible.

60. Best motto, Semper Fidelis, always faithful.

61. Mustang officers. Been there, done that.

62. Respect. The State Department chose Marines, not soldiers, to protect our embassies.

Steve Elfers

63. When the Marines found themselves surrounded by Chinese troops near the "Frozen Chosin" during the Korean War, a Marine officer summed it up for his men. "Good. Now I can shoot in all directions."

64. General Charles Krulak's Planning Guidance.

65. Being Officer of the Day.

66. Sgt. Maj. Leonard Koontz. As of 1996, he's the only enlisted Marine on active duty to wear the Navy Cross.

67. Annual leave. Thirty days of pure pleasure.

68. The Marine Air-Ground Task Force concept. Marines attack by land, by air and from the sea — simultaneously.

69. "The Commandant's Own," the Marine Corps Drum and Bugle Corps.

"Each year the company I work for, Litton Data Systems, holds a Marine Corps birthday luncheon so that former Marines who work here can celebrate their heritage. We have a Marine officer as a guest speaker, play the commandant's annual birthday message, and go through the formal cake cutting ceremony.

Even though most of us have been retired from the Corps for many years, we still feel like we are part of the Marine family, and events like this strengthen our ties to the Corps.

Being a part of such a large family is why I love the Marine Corps."

— Lt. Col. Anthony J. Garcia, USMC (Ret.); Covina, Calif.

70. “Can-do” spirit. Marines do more with less, and they like it that way.

71. Advance pay.

72. The Marine Corps University at Quantico. Believe it or not, the Corps has its own campus.

73. Field coffee, AKA 'Hobo Coffee.' Get a 15-gallon pot, 15 gallons of water, five pounds of coffee, and you're good to go.

74. No matter their skin color, all Marines bleed green.

75. MCI. Not long distance phone calls, but long distance learning.

76. Best haircut. Hands down. You can't have a bad hair day with a high and tight. And you spend less on shampoo.

77. Retired Col. John Bourgeois, the leader of the Marine Band for 28 years.

78. Reenlistment bonuses.

79. Mess night etiquette. Enter covered and drinks are on you.

80. The F4U Corsair. The Corps' sleek, gull-winged World War II warbird.

81. The 29 living Marines who wear the Medal of Honor, as of 1996.

82. Best service emblem: The Eagle, Globe and Anchor.

83. Respect. It follows you throughout your life once people discover you were a Marine.

84. Guard mount.

85. Nicknames. "Jarhead."

86. Nicknames. "Leatherneck."

87. Nicknames. "Gyrene."

88. Nicknames. "Devil Dog." Trivia question: Where did this term come from? Answer: The German Army in World War II, whose soldiers' greatest fear at the Battle of Belleau Wood was running up against the toughest American fighting men, the Marines. They called them "teufelhunden," or Devil Dogs.

89. Everyone's a Marine - officer and enlisted alike.

90. John Wayne. He should have been a Marine, but his Marine movies are good enough.

91. Sun Tzu. He shoulda been a Marine, too.

92. The Commandant's Reading List. Hemmingway it ain't, but RIFLEMAN DODD is still a great read.

93. The Marine Corps Historical Foundation.

94. The DI creed.

95. Unit guidons.

Chris Lawson

96. Mud. You wanna see pure joy? Look at a Marine after a wet day in the field.

97. The First Sergeants Course. You have to go back to school to wear the diamond.

98. MCX - the best exchanges in the military.

99. Congress loves the Corps. Some of the congressional "Mafia" of former Marines now in positions of power or influence over the defense budget include: Rep. Ronald Dellums (D-Calif.), Sen. John Glenn (D-Ohio), Sen. Chuck Robb (D-Va.), Rep. John Murtha (D-Pa.), Sen. John Warner (R-Va.)

100. Pride. After the 1982 Beirut bombing, Marine Corps Commandant Gen. P.X. Kelly visited a wounded Marine in the hospital to present him his Purple Heart medal. Covered by tubes and unable to speak, the Marine simply asked for pad and pen. On it he wrote: "Semper Fi."

101. The Corps' first recruiting station: Tun Tavern, Philadelphia, 1775. It was a bar, no less.

"My reason for loving the Marine Corps is not because of the colorful, winning history of the Corps. It's not because my granddad was a Marine. It's not because my dad was a Marine. It's not because my little brother was a Marine. It's not even because I was a Marine.

You see, I'm in the Coast Guard these days, and every day the Marine Corps influences how I am. Everything from how I wear my uniform to how I train and lead my subordinates reflects both the Coast Guard and the Marine Corps. I believe that when the Coast Guard got me, they got a pretty good deal, compliments of the Corps."

— MK1 Bill Wilson: USCG Loran Station, WA

102. Most respected service. When Marines pulled out of Somalia in 1995, the media reported the U.S. military was pulling out — as if tens of thousands of Army troops weren't still in the country. Now that's respect.

103. Chesty IV. In 1995, this bulldog was tapped to be the Corps' first female mascot.

104. The Commissary.

105. Best motivational war-cry: Ooh-rah!

106. War dogs. Marines with a bite!

107. "1775 Rum Punch" - four parts dark rum, two parts lime juice, one part pure maple syrup. Grenadine to taste.

108. Arlington National Cemetery. The final resting place for great Marines like Maj. Gen. John A. Lejeune.

109. Force Recon.

110. Tiger cruises.

111. Making your first cutting score.

112. The Continental Marines. The "really" Old Corps.

113. The Commandant's House. It's the oldest occupied residence in Washington, D.C.

114. LtGen. Carol A. Mutter. She's one of two women in the United States military to currently wear three stars. The other: VAdm. Patricia Tracey.

115. "A ship without Marines is like a coat without buttons." — Adm. David G. Farragut.

116. "The Continental ship Providence, now lying at Boston, is bound on a short cruise, immediately; a few good men are wanted to make her compliment."

— Marine Capt. William Jones, from a want ad in the PROVIDENCE (R.I.) GAZETTE, March 20, 1779.

117. Boss' night. Every so often, the NCOs or staff NCOs buy the drinks for their charges at their club. Can't beat that!

118. Dive Pay. Flight Pay. Hazard Duty Pay.

119. Physical fitness. You've seen portly chiefs, but there are no fat Marines.

120. It's a cover, not a hat. Hats are for Zoomies.

121. Fitness Reports. Good ones, that is.

122. .50 caliber sniper rifles. Ooh-rah!

123. Riverine Assault Craft. RAC Attack.

"Marines don't wear a scruffy uniform.
Marines don't slouch around with their hands in their pockets.
Marines don't wear long hair.
Marines don't fail to respond with a 'yes or no, sir' when speaking with a senior.
Marines don't gang up on each other.
Marines don't question lawful orders.
Marines don't lie or cheat or break their word.
Marines don't abandon a fellow Marine in time of need
Marines don't let down their fellow Marines by succumbing to drug temptation.
Marines don't meet problems with 'It can't be done' or questions with the easy answer 'no.'"

— L.F. Chapman, Jr.; Commandant, 1968-71

124. Air power. When the grunts look to the sky for support, they see flying Leathernecks, not Zoomies.

125. Hollywood loves the Marines. A few examples: "Sands of Iwo Jima," "The Wind and the Lion," "Heartbreak Ridge," "The Flying Leathernecks," "The DI," and "Death Before Dishonor."

126. And television loves Marines, too. "Baa Baa Black Sheep," "Gomer Pyle, USMC," and "Major Dad."

127. When asked by the press, an overseas Marine doesn't say, "I don't know what the mission is," "I don't know why I'm here" and "I don't like it here." A Marine knows. It's his calling.

128. Dog and pony shows.

129. The only official, congressionally sanctioned hymn for any of the services. "The Marines' Hymn."

FROM THE HALLS OF MONTEZUMA,
TO THE SHORES OF TRIPOLI;
WE FIGHT OUR COUNTRY'S BATTLES
IN THE AIR, ON LAND, AND SEA;
FIRST TO FIGHT FOR RIGHT AND FREEDOM
AND TO KEEP OUR HONOR CLEAN;
WE ARE PROUD TO CLAIM THE TITLE OF
UNITED STATES MARINE.

130. The “docs,” - Marines’ corpsmen-in-arms. They’re sailors, but they’re as tough as the Marines they care for. In World War I alone, Navy corpsmen were awarded seven Medals of Honor, 69 Navy Crosses and 486 Silver Stars.

131. First in orbit. No, that’s not another gunny losing his temper. John Glenn, that clean Marine, was the first American to orbit Earth. Now he’s a veteran senator.

132. Best description: Soldiers of the Sea.

133. The genesis of the USMC emblem:

We stole the Eagle from the Air Force,
The Anchor from the Navy,
The Rope from the Army,
And on the seventh day when God rested,
We overran His perimeter and stole the Globe
And have been running the show ever since.

—Author Unknown

134. When the President climbs into a helicopter, he flies Marine One.

135. Inspections.

136. Slopchutes.

137. Teamwork. Gotta have it. Gotta love it.

138. Core values: Courage, Honor, Commitment.

139. The Mameluke Sword.

"There are four kinds of Marines: those in Saudi Arabia, those going to Saudi Arabia, those who want to go to Saudi Arabia, and those who don't want to go but are going anyway."

- Gen. Al Gray,
Commandant of the Marine Corps
during Operation Desert Storm

140. Amphibians one and all. Like the Army, the Corps has armored vehicles. But the Marines' not only fight, they swim.

141. Because the Corps is so small, you get to see your friends over and over and over.

142. If you don't like your neighbors, you know you'll be moving in a few years.

143. Starch. Nothing beats a pair of starched cammies.

144. Lifers.

145. Short-timers.

146. Marines symbolize: discipline, courage, honor, commitment, valor, patriotism, and military virtue.

147. Birthday traditions, like seeing who's the oldest and youngest Marine in your unit.

148. The NCO creed.

149. Sgt. Maj. of the Marine Corps Lewis G. Lee. You gotta love the straight talk from the Corps' top dog. And his wife is a Marine too.

150. The seabag. A virtual floating footlocker.

151. The Command and Staff College Foundation.

152. Coming home from deployment.

153. The "People's Own" Marine Corps Marathon.

154. The bus ride onto Parris Island. It's literally the ride of a lifetime.

USMC Photo

155. SPIE Rigging. Up, up and away.

156. Sub-Marines.

157. The Navy Relief Society.

158. Mud races and volksmarches.

159. Brain Games: The Commandant's Warfighting Lab.

160. Marinettes.

"I fell in love with the Marines when my brother, Christopher (now a Reserve captain) became one. The Marines gave shape and meaning to his young life and made him a part of a tradition he could be truly proud of. Though it never occurred to me to join up myself, my brother has given me an extra special connection to the Corps.

Shortly after he came back from the Persian Gulf, he helped me fight my own battle with leukemia, donating his own bone marrow for a transplant that saved my life. We call it the Mighty Marine Marrow and it continues to keep the enemy at bay. I guess that makes me an auxiliary Marine. Semper Fi."

— Laura Landro; New York, N.Y.

161. First on foot and right of the line. Marines form at the place of honor in any naval formation. The Secretary of the Navy bestowed that honor in 1876.

162. There are two kinds of people in the world: Marines and those who wish they were.

163. God created man; the U.S. Marine Corps fine-tunes them.

164. Qual Day on the rifle range.

165. Rack Monsters.

166. Military funerals.

167. Fighting style. When the U.S. went into Haiti in 1994, Army soldiers sought cover behind their rucksacks. Marines DUG IN!

168. "Uncommon valor was a common virtue."
— Adm. Chester Nimitz, commander of Pacific forces in World War II.

169. Unity. Ultimately, everyone joins for the same basic reason: To be a United States Marine.

170. Semper Gumby. Always flexible.

171. Your first NCO promotion warrant.

172. Retired Commandant Gen. Carl E. Mundy, Jr. A warrior with class. And he saved the Corps' soul — its people — during the 1994 drawdown.

173. Travel. So many countries, so little time.

174. NJP. Someone else's, that is.

175. Those Knights-in-Shining-Armor commercials.

176. Navy chaplains. You gotta love a man of the cloth when the cloth is camouflaged.

177. The Marines' Memorial Club in downtown San Francisco. Sleeping in style for $55 a night.

178. OCS.

179. Tradition. The Corps is older than the Republic itself!

180. Joe Rosenthal's famous flag-raising shot at Iwo Jima. An icon for the Corps and an inspiration for a country.

181. Terminology. In the Corps, it's a "fighting" hole, not a "fox" hole. Fox holes are for people who want to hide. Fighting holes are for people who want to fight.

182. Hogan's Alley. Urban training with a twist.

"I have never been so proud of myself than on boot camp Graduation Day. What a feeling."

— Ron Teed; Pontiac, Michigan

183. You learn you can do things you once thought impossible, like making that 15-mile hump, or running that 6.2 miles, or jumping from that perfectly good airplane.

184. Jane Wayne days.

185. Wetting-down parties. No one celebrates promotions with more flair and admiration.

186. When the Navy needed someone to guard its ships, sailors and nuclear devices, they called on Marines.

USMC Photo

187. Best military monument: The Marine Corps War Memorial, better known as the Iwo Jima Monument.

188. Parades. Strutting your stuff.

189. Show of Pride: Marines have the most stickers spotted on America's highways on car bumpers and windows.

190. The Marine Corps verse of the "Navy Hymn":

Eternal Father grant we pray,
To all Marines both night and day,
The courage, honor, strength and skill
Their land to serve, thy law fulfill;
Be thou the shield forevermore
From every peril to the Corps.

191. Challenges. Proving you have the mettle to be a Marine.

192. "Come on, you sons of bitches! Do you want to live forever?" — Sgt. Dan Daly, World War I.

193. Retirement ceremonies. Going out in style.

194. Great recruiting slogans: "Send in the Marines."

195. Legendary Marine sniper GySgt. Carlos Hathcock. He had 93 confirmed kills in Vietnam.

196. The Quarterdeck.

197. Best personalized license plate: "1775." It's always on the commandant's car.

198. Smedley D. Butler. With a name like Smedley, he had to be tough. From the Philippines to Haiti, he was an expert suppressing revolution. His blunt style was pure Marine.

199. The 1MC. What a way to start the day.

200. At a dinner after he left office, George Bush said, "The thing I miss most about being President is the Marine Band." Then President Clinton said, "The thing I like most about being President is the Marine Band." (From PARADE MAGAZINE.)

201. Combat correspondents. They're journalists in the Navy, but in the Corps, the job is combat correspondents, thank you very much.

202. The Blue Angels. Marine jet jocks fly with the best.

203. Capt. Marion E. Carl (VMF-223.) The Corps' first ace with 18.5 kills in WWI.

"I think mostly it's the commitment to the Corps. Everybody, from the wives to the children, all of them are proud to be a part of it. I know it's been my life for 60 years and I wouldn't give it up for anything. It's been hard — five times, people I love went off to war. But they all came back, so I guess that makes me the luckiest woman in the entire United States of America!"

— Amy Krulak, mother of Marine Corps Commandant Gen. Charles C. Krulak, Jr.

Mrs. Krulak, 84, who is married to retired Lt. Gen. Victor "Brute" Krulak, was asked in 1995 to describe her husband in just one word. Her answer: "Sexy." Yet another reason to love the Corps.

204. The British Royal Marines. Brothers in Arms.

205. "The Marines have landed and have the situation well in hand." — Richard Harding Davis.

206. China Marines.

207. Proceed Time.

208. Earning the title. The right to be called a Marine.

209. Fast-roping. The quickest way to the deck.

210. The Delta Corridor at Twentynine Palms.

211. 782 gear.

212. "Manila John" Basilone. A true gunfighter from the word go. The first enlisted Marine in World War II to be awarded the Medal of Honor. He got it for his heroic efforts on Guadalcanal. Later killed on Iwo Jima, and posthumously awarded the Navy Cross.

213. The MP-5 submachine gun. A warrior's dream machine.

214. The Young Marines Program. Community service at its best.

215. Cobras. Snakes in the sky.

216. Sergeants Major. You better love 'em.

217. Esprit de Corps. Even if you can't spell or pronounce it, the Marine Corps has it in spades. An example: When sailors get tattoos, they do it to express their individuality, and their choices range from Betty Boop and Mickey Mouse to raging sea serpents. When Marines get tattoos, they do it to express their solidarity, and choose bulldogs, "Death Before Dishonor," and "USMC."

218. Marine raids. They epitomize shock, surprise and violence.

219. A Few Good Men. And a Few Very Good Women.

220. Field expedient. The Marine way.

221. "Casualities many; percentage of dead not known; combat efficiency: we are winning."
— Col. David M. Shoup, battlefield dispatch from Tarawa; Nov. 21, 1943.

USMC Photo

222. The Friday evening parade at 8th and I Barracks in Washington. The best show in town.

223. The Tuesday night Sunset Parade at the Iwo Jima Memorial. Less formal, just as exciting, and you can't beat the view.

224. The Sergeant's Course. Grooming the next generation.

225. Friends. You meet them coming and going. And they're always there to help you move.

226. Water survival training. Just ask LCpl. Zachary Mayo, who fell off the aircraft carrier America in 1995 and lived to tell about it.

227. Cumshaw.

228. The Beirut Memorial at Camp Lejeune, N.C. A stirring tribute to the 220 Marines, 18 Navy corpsman, and three soldiers who were killed in the bombing of the Marine Barracks in Beirut, Lebanon. A stand of trees. A statue of bronze. A simple wall of honor.

229. Your first medal.

"I had a recruiter tell me before I signed up, 'It's not like the Army's 'BE ALL YOU CAN BE.' In the Marine Corps, it's 'GIVE ALL YOU GOT!' "

- LCpl. F.H. Winston, 24th Marines

230. USO shows.

231. The Marine Military Academy.

232. LINE training. Hand to hand at its best.

233. The Corps' triple play: shooting, moving and communicating.

234. When the Air Force deploys, they carry their Samsonite bags on luggage carriers and stay in hotels. When Marines deploy, it's two seabags and your weapons. And a tent in the bush.

235. "Good night, Chesty, wherever you are."

236. The 11 General Orders. (Go on, name 'em.)

237. TBS. Infantrymen all.

238. That's Marines, with a capital M.

239. All that Marine speak. It's the Head, not the Bathroom; It's a Hatch, not a Door; It's a Cover, not a Hat; It's an Overhead, not a Ceiling; It's a Bulkhead, not a Wall.

240. "The President's Own," the Marine Corps Band.

241. John Philip Sousa, "The March King," the world famous bandmaster, was the first leader of the band.

242. "You don't hurt 'em if you don't hit 'em."
— Lt. Gen. Lewis B. "Chesty" Puller.

243. Best duty assignments: Okinawa, Kaneohe Bay, Camp Pendleton, Diego Garcia, Moscow, North Carolina. Plus any ship at sea.

244. Worst duty assignments: Okinawa, Kaneohe Bay, Camp Pendleton, Diego Garcia, Moscow, North Carolina. Plus any ship at sea.

245. True heroes. The 40,000 Marines who have given their lives on the fields of battle since the Revolutionary War.

246. The scarlet stripe on NCO and officer trousers. They're not just sharp, they serve a point: The stripes represent blood shed in battle.

247. Unity. Every Marine is first and foremost a rifleman. Officer and enlisted alike.

248. The Corporal's Course. Professional training for young NCOs.

249. Family days.

250. Great recruiting slogans: "We don't promise you a rose garden."

251. The Marines have done so much with so little for so long that they are now qualified to do anything with nothing.

252. Marine Gunners. Bursting bombs and all.

USMC Photo

253. Most remarkable airplane: The AV-8B Harrier jump jet. No other service's jets can take off and land on a dime.

254. First in, last out.

255. Command and Staff College. Tough but tactical.

256. You won't hear much whining come deployment time. Most Marines want to be where the action is.

257. Gen. Archibald Henderson, the "Grand Old Man" of the Corps. He was commandant for 39 years (1820-1859).

258. When it absolutely, positively, has to be destroyed overnight, send in the Marines!

259. Pride. When you're the best, it's hard to imagine being part of the rest.

260. Only military branch with a beer named in its honor: Tun Tavern Beer.

261. Bravado. A Marine quote from the Gulf War: "I sure hope the Iraqis are good lovers, because they sure can't fight."

262. Per diem.

"I currently serve in an Army airborne unit. I like the gutsy thing of jumping out of perfectly good aircraft, but God, do I miss the Corps. The Army doesn't have the brotherhood, traditions, discipline, or I dare say, the honor that the Marine Corps has instilled in me. Once a Marine, always a Marine."

— P. Woods, North Carolina

263. The rifle range. Where else can you get the billet of "Butts NCO."

264. During a recent joint exercise a Navy admiral repeatedly called a veteran Marine master sergeant "chief," the Navy's equivalent rank. On the last day of the operation, the admiral caught himself again calling the Marine "chief" and said, "I'm sorry, master sergeant, but if you were in the Navy, you would be a chief."
"No sir," the Marine replied. "If I were in the Navy, I'd be an admiral."

265. The recipe for a Marine wife:
1 1/2 cups patience
1 cup courage
3/4 cup tolerance
1 pound ability
2 tablespoons elbow grease
dash of adventure
Add above ingredients together. Let set alone for many months. Marinate frequently with salty tears. Pour off excess fat. Sprinkle ever so lightly with money. Knead dough until payday. Season with international spices. Bake 20 years or until done. Serve with pride.

– Author unknown

266. Marine spouses. God love ‘em. They have it the worst of any of the other service spouses. They endure six-month deployments and one- and two-year unaccompanied tours. The ones who survive a career are as tough as the Marines they married.

267. Marine kids. God love them more. They know the meaning of duty, honor and country at too young an age.

268. Marine Raiders. The original Special Forces.

269. The Quonset Hut. Believe it or not, they're still around and in use.

270. Being frocked.

271. Marines who went to Hollywood. Among them: Don Adams, Charlton Heston, Bob Keeshan (Captain Kangaroo), Lee Marvin, Steve McQueen, Burt Reynolds, George C. Scott, Gene Hackman.

272. Tax advantages. VHA and BAQ — your housing allowances — are tax-free.

273. Tax advantages. You don't pay tax at the exchange either.

274. The Marine Corps Museum at the Washington Navy Yard. It houses the flag raised on Iwo Jima and other icons of the Corps.

275. Australia. In 1997, Devil Dogs may be headed "Down Under" for training.

276. Camp Swampy. Sand fleas and all.

Phil Thompson

277. The Birthday Ball.

278. "From the Trenches," the humor of former Capt. Phil Thompson, Navy Times Marine cartoonist.

279. Global presence, global reach. As the Hymn notes, so spread out are Marines around the globe that some can watch the sun set while others are watching it rise.

280. Former Commandant Gen. Al Gray's official portrait: in cammies.

281. Former Commandant Gen. Al Gray's coffee mug: a four-star canteen cup.

282. Best fighting knife: The Ka-Bar.
     Blood groove and all.

283. Your first commission.

284. Marines don't just read about history,
     they make it.

285. The Good Conduct Medal, also known as the infamous "didn't get caught" medal.

286. The Gunny's salty sea stories.

"Everyone knows the saying 'love the man, love the Corps.' When I married my husband, I came from a military family and saw no particular essence to this saying. Over the years, however, I have seen a powerful bond within the Corps that brings distinct meaning to the 'band of brothers.'

"After my husband was killed, a circumstance that could turn a wife away, the men and women of the Corps have remained "forever faithful" to me. The fact that the Corps is still there for me helps keep him close. The esprit de corps keeps him constantly alive."

— Sue Davis, widow of Brig. Gen. Jerry Cowan
Oceanside, CA

287. Your D.I.s. You'll never forget their names. Go on...remember?

288. You learn to overcome fears, or risk letting the Corps and your fellow Marines down. In the end, everyone wins!

289. Mess night etiquette. Those who make the most pay the most.

290. The officer's Sam Browne Belt.

291. Toys for Tots. Santa Corps.

292. Relevance. Civilian business leaders are so impressed with Fleet Marine Force Manual 1, "Warfighting," that they are using it to hone their skills for boardroom battles.

293. The Staff NCOs. The Keepers of the flame.

294. The Marines invade, then go home. The Army usually does the occupying.

295. The French Fourragere, awarded for Belleau Wood.

296. Despite their service to U.S. presidents, no Marine has ever been president. Now that's smart!

297. Good taste in gifts. Wanna know how much a Marine missed his family during a deployment? Check out the china and toys in his seabag on the return trip, and then look at his credit card bill.

298. The 1st and 15th of each month. Gotta pay for all those good gifts.

299. Being the pointy tip of America's spear, out in front, kicking down the door. What the Marines do best.

300. Mail call. From boot camp to the fleet, you can't survive without it.

301. "Leading Marines," a classic textbook in leadership.

Steve Elfers

302. The taste of SOS in the morning.

303. Marine snipers. One shot, one kill, one thousand yards.

304. Libbo. Anytime, anywhere.

305. Leadership. In the Corps, Lance Corporals and Corporals do more than most E-6s in other branches.

306. November 10. You get two birthdays a year.

"When my best friend, Bill Price, left for Parris Island, he was a confused, directionless kid. When I visited 13 weeks later, I was thrilled and amazed at the difference in him.

"His hair was high and tight. He'd lost almost 30 pounds. He looked great in his graduation uniform. But the difference was more than just his looks. The biggest difference was inside — his attitude. He had become a man. He had learned honor, integrity and respect. He finally knew who he was. He was bursting with pride in being Pfc. Price, Marine. For transforming the boys of America into proud men, thank you USMC!"

— Kirk Kimball; Mamaroneck, N.Y.

307. Non-Comms rate their own ceremonial sword. The Marines are the only branch to have them.

308. Women Marines. They've earned their place in the ranks and serve with distinction.

309. Because not everyone can be a Marine.
Do you have what it takes?

310. Maj. A.A. Cunningham, the father of
Marine Corps aviation.

311. Amphibious Warfare School. Getting selected is
half the battle.

312. Capt. Samuel Nicholas. The Corps' first commissioned officer and commandant.

313. Toughest DIs. They're so tough that when the Navy wants to train its officers, who do they call? 1-800-MARINES.

314. The Air Force. Aren't you glad you're not an airman? They're pampered, yet they still find time to whine.

315. The Army. They get the best equipment first and the Marines still do it better.

316. The Navy. Give them credit. They have it almost as tough as Marines. But who wants to be a limo service?

317. The Coast Guard. Tell the truth: If you couldn't be a Marine, would you be a Coastie? In those powder blue uniforms? Not on your life!

318. “Retreat...Hell! We just got here.” — Col. Wendell “Whispering Buck” Neville, fighting in France during World War I.

319. Dunk’s Almanac.

"The Corps is a family in good times and in bad times. A home-cooked meal waited for us when we came home from the hospital with our first child."

— Arlene Arzola-Kloch,
wife of Marine Capt. Michael L. Kloch;
NAS Meridian, CA

320. The silent drill platoon. Just watching them ply their trade makes you want to sign up.

321. The Rifleman's Creed.

322. No smiling in official portraits. All business.

USMC Photo

323. Chesty Puller. It's more than the name. He started in the Corps with a reserve commission and was released in the drawdown after World War I. He then enlisted as a corporal, served in Haiti and received his second commission in 1924. He retired in 1955 a lieutenant general, the most decorated Marine in history, and probably the most colorful as well.

324. The ONLY combined arms force. You want jointness? The Marine Corps has been joint for decades, with its own air force, groundpounders and navy in one.

325. Navy ships christened in honor of Marine battles. They include: Inchon, Belleau Wood, Guadalcanal and others.

"I have an affinity for the Corps. My dad was a Marine. He grew up in Baltimore, at St. Mary's Orphanage. At 16 he ran away, fortunately, to find his first real home — the Marine Corps. The Corps became the family he had never known.

He survived the Frozen Chosin. He survived civilian life because of the strong sense of self-worth the Marines instilled in him. He survived fatherhood because the Corps taught him accountability and family. What he couldn't survive was a massive heart attack at the age of 42.

True to form, the Corps was the first to respond when dad died. They helped my mother pay burial expenses.

My dad, Thomas S. Smith Sr., was once, and always, a Marine."

— Christine A. Hield; Halethorpe, Md.

326. Expediency: "First to Fight."

327. Marines are winners. Consider, for example: Tarawa, Saipan, Guadalcanal, Tripoli, Belleau Wood, Chosin, Hue City, Peleliu, Leyte Gulf, Guam, Tinian, Iwo Jima and Okinawa.

Chris Lawson

328. Training. The more you sweat in peace, the less you bleed in war.

329. Innovative thinking, both past and present. Examples: the Landing Craft; the AAAV; the MV-22 Osprey; and the Harrier.

330. Sunsets in the Twentynine Palms desert.

Contributors

SSgt. John D. Arvin, Wally Beddoe, Mark Camp, LCpl. Michael E. Cook, T. Curtis, John M. Fielding, Lincoln Gardner, MSgt. Gerald R. Hall (Ret.), Sgt. Christopher M. Hayes, Lt. Denise P. Marsden, Ru Schmitt, Jeff Stevenson, GySgt. Gregory A. Threat, Lt. Col. F. Phil Torres, L.T. Twomey, Laddie J. Vacek, Jim Westbrook and Melissa Williams.

About the Author

Lawson then...

Chris Lawson is a staff writer for Navy Times and has covered the activities of Marines and sailors worldwide since December, 1992.

A former Marine Corps Combat Correspondent, Lawson left the Corps as a sergeant in 1991 to pursue a career as a defense reporter. During his six years in the Corps, Lawson was named the Marine Corps Print Journalist of the Year, and was a runner-up in the Military Journalist of the Year Competition in 1989.

...and now.

Lawson is a graduate of the Military Photojournalism Program at Syracuse University, and currently lives in Alexandria, Va.

His military decorations include the Navy Commendation Medal, the Navy Achievement Medal (w/Gold Star), the Meritorious Unit Commendation Medal, the Good Conduct Medal and the National Defense Service Medal.